Stalking the Perfect Tan

Doonesbury books by G. B. Trudeau

Still a Few Bugs in the System
The President Is a Lot Smarter Than You Think
But This War Had Such Promise
Call Me When You Find America
Guilty, Guilty, Guilty!
"What Do We Have for the Witnesses, Johnnie?"
Dare To Be Great, Ms. Caucus
Wouldn't a Gremlin Have Been More Sensible?
"Speaking of Inalienable Rights, Amy . . ."
You're Never Too Old for Nuts and Berries
An Especially Tricky People
As the Kid Goes for Broke
Stalking the Perfect Tan
"Any Grooming Hints for Your Fans, Rollie?"
But the Pension Fund Was Just Sitting There
We're Not Out of the Woods Yet
A Tad Overweight, but Violet Eyes to Die For
And That's My Final Offer!
He's Never Heard of You, Either

In Large Format

The Doonesbury Chronicles
Doonesbury's Greatest Hits

a Doonesbury classic by

G.B. Trudeau.

Stalking the Perfect Tan

An Owl Book   Henry Holt and Company / New York

Library of Congress Catalog Card Number: 77-15206
ISBN: 0-8050-0470-X

Printed in the United States of America

The cartoons in this book have appeared in newspapers
in the United States and abroad under the auspices of
Universal Press Syndicate.

10 9 8 7

ISBN 0-8050-0470-X

I REALLY DON'T UNDERSTAND WHY YOU'RE SO KEEN ON GOING TO THIS PARTY, LACEY..

WELL, FOR ONE THING, DICK, THE ENTIRE CARTER CABINET WILL PROBABLY BE THERE!

THAT'S A **DRAW**?! THE CARTER CABINET IS THE MOST BIZARRE COLLECTION OF CRONIES, RETREADS AND TOKENS EVER ASSEMBLED!

I KNOW THAT, DEAR, BUT I'M NEW IN TOWN! I WANT A CHANCE TO SIZE UP THE PEOPLE IN CHARGE!

OKAY, BUT WHY DO I HAVE TO GO? WHO'S GOING TO WANT TO TALK TO AN ELDERLY ORNITHOLOGIST?

ME. IN 35 YEARS, I'VE NEVER BEEN TO A PARTY WHERE YOU WEREN'T THE MOST FASCINATING PERSON THERE.

OH.

KEEP YOUR EYES ON THE ROAD, DRIVER.

YES'M.

GBTrudeau

A FINAL WORD TO THE WISE, EVERYONE: WHEN REPORTING SALARIES, **ALWAYS** TELL IT LIKE IT IS! IT'S TIME WE STOPPED USING EUPHEMISMS LIKE "A SIX-FIGURE INCOME"!

LET'S SAY YOUR SUBJECT EARNS "A SIX-FIGURE INCOME". DOES THAT MEAN HE MAKES $100,000, OR $900,000? THIS IS A **VERY** IMPORTANT DISTINCTION TO OUR READERS!

I SAY, LET'S CALL A $100,000 SALARY $100,000, AND A $900,000 SALARY $900,000!

YEEAA! YEA!

HEAR! HEAR!

CLAP! CLAP! CLAP! CLAP!

THANK YOU. I'VE BEEN ASKED TO REMIND YOU THAT THE JACKIE O. RETROSPECTIVE WILL RESUME AT THREE.

WE'LL BE COVERING THE GREEK YEARS TODAY, PEOPLE!

GBTrudeau

..AND THEN WHEN THEY GOT TO THE SCENE WHERE KUNTA KINTE IS CAPTURED, CLYDE JUST WENT INTO A FIT OF RAGE!

WELL, IT WAS A PRETTY DIS-TURBING SHOW, GINNY..

I KNOW, BUT I'VE NEVER SEEN CLYDE SO SHAKEN!

THE WHOLE WEEK "ROOTS" WAS ON, HE JUST WALKED AROUND IN A DAZE SAYING OVER AND OVER, "WHO AM I? HOW DID I GET HERE?"

BUT CLYDE ALWAYS SAYS THAT!

I KNOW, BUT THIS TIME IT REALLY WORRIED ME..

GOOD EVENING. TODAY THE PRESIDENT CREATED A NEW ADMINISTRATION POST — SECRETARY OF SYMBOLISM. OUR MAN CAROL SIMPSON WAS THERE.

TO ADMINISTRATION TOPSIDERS, IT CAME AS NO SURPRISE TODAY THAT CARTER PICKED DUANE DELACOURT TO BE HIS NEW SYMBOLISM CHIEF. HE WAS, AFTER ALL, THE MAN BEHIND THE CARDIGAN, THE CHAT, THE STROLL, AND THE PUBLIC EDUCATION OF AMY!

THE SECRETARY-DESIGNATE IS NOTHING IF NOT PROLIFIC. DELACOURT HAS ALREADY ANNOUNCED THAT A MAJOR SYMBOLIC GESTURE WILL TAKE PLACE TONIGHT AT 9:00 P.M. EASTERN STANDARD TIME.

NBC NEWS WILL, OF COURSE, BE PROVIDING LIVE COVERAGE OF THE GESTURE. FOR CAPITOL HILL REACTION, THIS FROM OUR MAN LINDA ELLERBEE..

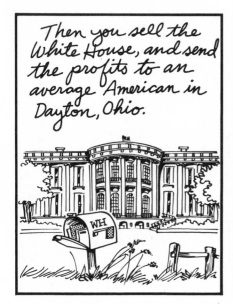

MR. DELACOURT, MY POINT IS THAT JIMMY CARTER HAS HAD **YEARS** OF PUBLIC SERVICE TO FIND OUT WHAT'S ON THE MINDS OF THE AMERICAN PEOPLE!

IF THE PRESIDENT DOESN'T KNOW WHAT THE NEEDS OF THE COUNTRY ARE BY NOW, HE'S **NEVER** GOING TO KNOW!

SENATOR, AS I SAID BEFORE, IT'S REALLY A QUESTION OF KEEPING IN TOUCH..

KEEPING IN **TOUCH?!** MR. DELACOURT, THE MAN NEVER LET **GO!** FIVE MONTHS AFTER THE ELECTION, HE'S **STILL** CAMPAIGNING!

WELL, WE FEEL VOTERS APPRECIATE THE FACT HE CARES ENOUGH TO CAMPAIGN AFTER THE ELECTION AS WELL.

BUT, DUANE! HE **WON!** HE **WON** THE ELECTION!

I KNOW. I STILL CAN'T BELIEVE IT. IT'S LIKE A DREAM, Y'KNOW?

GOOD EVENING. TODAY, BY A NARROW MARGIN OF 50 TO 46, THE U.S. SENATE CONFIRMED DUANE DELACOURT AS THE NEW SECRETARY OF SYMBOLISM! CATHERINE MACKIN HAS MORE. CASSIE?

THANK YOU, JOHN. I'M HERE IN THE WHITE HOUSE BRIEFING ROOM WITH SECRETARY-ELECT DUANE DELACOURT. THE MOOD HERE IS ONE OF TRIUMPH, IS IT NOT, MR. SECRETARY?

YES. THAT'S RIGHT..

IT'S A MOMENT OF PERSONAL TRIUMPH, OF COURSE, BUT MORE IMPORTANTLY, IT IS A VICTORY FOR SYMBOLISM—FOR CARDIGANS, FOR TOWN MEETINGS, FOR CALL-IN SHOWS AND FOR FIRESIDE CHATS!

YES, IT'S A VICTORY FOR THE "LITTLE GUY," THE "MAN IN THE STREET," THE "AVERAGE JOE"...

BACK TO YOU, JOHN, IF YOU DON'T MIND.

GBTrudeau

..AND AS YOU WILL SEE TONIGHT, NO NATION HAS A MONOPOLY ON HUMAN RIGHTS! THE NOMINEES RANGE FROM THE SMALLEST ISLAND DOMAIN IN THE SOUTH PACIFIC TO THE LARGEST INDUSTRIAL POWER IN EUROPE!

YES, ANY COUNTRY OBSERVING THE U.N.'S 13 FUNDAMENTAL RIGHTS IS ELIGIBLE FOR ONE OF THESE HANDSOME HUMAN RIGHTS TROPHIES WE'LL SOON BE PRESENTING!

AND JUST WHAT ARE THOSE RIGHTS? WELL, ON THE BACK OF YOUR MENUS, YOU'LL FIND A SAMPLE SCORECARD WITH THE WHOLE LIST! EVERYTHING FROM DUE PROCESS TO PROTECTION FROM PERSONAL VIOLENCE!

SO DURING DINNER, GO AHEAD — RATE YOURSELF! IT'S EASY AND FUN! GOOD LUCK TO ALL!

GBTrudeau

TRY TO UNDERSTAND, BRENDA, I WOULD'VE QUIT ANYWAY! HOW MUCH LONGER DID YOU THINK I COULD CONTINUE WORKING FOR A MAGAZINE THAT REFLECTS SUCH HOPELESSLY BANAL VALUES?

DON'T YOU SEE WHAT YOU'RE DOING, BRENDA? THE MESSAGE OF "PEOPLE" IS NOT SO MUCH THAT EVERYONE **CAN** BE A STAR AS IT IS THAT EVERYONE SHOULD **WANT** TO BE A STAR! THAT'S JUST **CRAZY!**

＞SIGH＜.. THAT MAKES NO SENSE TO YOU WHATSOEVER, DOES IT? I MIGHT AS WELL BE TALKING TO THE TIME-LIFE BUILDING ITSELF..

WE'LL BE WANTING TO DEBRIEF YOU ON THE FONZ, OF COURSE.

YEAH..OKAY.. WHATEVER YOU SAY, BRENDA.

YOU KNOW, RICK, YOUR MENTIONING THE ETHICS COMMITTEE GOT ME THINKING. LACEY DAVENPORT'S ON THAT COMMITTEE. THINK SHE'D BE HIRING COUNSEL FOR THE KOREAN HEARINGS?

WELL, IT'S WORTH A TRY..

EXCEPT IT COULD BE RISKY. MAYBE SHE'S NOT ABOVE HARBORING POLITICAL GRUDGES, YOU KNOW?

I MEAN, WHAT IF SHE HIRES ME, AND THEN LEAKS SOMETHING AND BLAMES ME, AND THEN FIRES ME ON NATIONAL TELEVISION, *HUMILIATING* ME IN FRONT OF THE WHOLE COUNTRY?

YEAH, WHAT IF SHE DOES THAT?

I BETTER NOT CALL HER.

GBTrudeau

MS. CAUCUS, WHAT A DELIGHT TO HEAR FROM YOU! ARE YOU HERE IN WASHINGTON?

UM.. YES, I AM, MRS. DAVENPORT, JUST GOT IN, SO I THOUGHT, HECK, WHY NOT GIVE MY CONGRESSWOMAN A CALL, YOU KNOW, TO SHOW THERE WERE NO HARD FEELINGS ABOUT LAST FALL..

IN FACT, BOTH GINNY AND I FEEL IT WAS RATHER A PRIVILEGE TO RUN AGAINST YOU. IT WAS A CLEAN RACE, RIGHT? AND FREE OF ACRIMONY! AND..UH..**WELL** FOUGHT BY BOTH SIDES, DON'T YOU THINK?

YES, I GUESS IT WAS, DEAR..

LACEY, I NEED A JOB.

SO DID I, DEAR. BUT COME BY ANY-WAY.

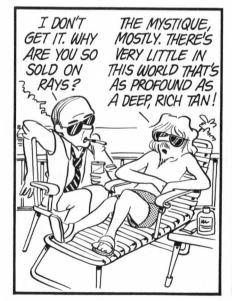

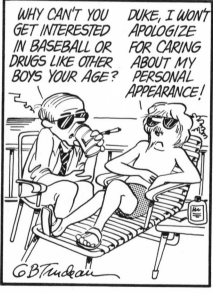